A Guide for Using

Loser

in the Classroom

Based on the novel written by Jerry Spinelli

This guide written by

Michael H. Levin, M.A., NBCT

Teacher Created Resources, Inc.
6421 Industry Way
Westminster, CA 92683
www.teachercreated.com

ISBN: 978-1-4206-2160-0

©2008 Teacher Created Resources, Inc.

Made in U.S.A.

Edited by
Heather Douglas

Illustrated by
Clint McKnight

Cover Art by
Courtney Barnes

Table of Contents

Introduction

A good book can touch our lives like a good friend. Within its pages are words and characters that can inspire us to achieve our highest ideals. We can turn to it for companionship, recreation, comfort, and guidance. It can also give us a cherished story to hold in our hearts forever.

In Literature Units, great care has been take to select books that are sure to become good friends!

Teachers who use this unit will find the following features to supplement their own valuable ideas.

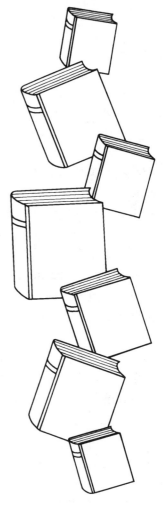

- Sample Lesson Plans
- Pre-reading Activities
- A Biographical Sketch and Picture of the Author
- A Book Summary
- Vocabulary Lists and Suggested Vocabulary Activities
- Chapters grouped for study, with each section including:
  —*quizzes*
  —*hands-on projects*
  —*cooperative learning activities*
  —*cross-curricular connections*
  —*extensions into the reader's own life*
- Post-reading Activities
- Book Report Ideas
- Research Activities
- Culminating Activities
- Three Different Options for Unit Tests
- A Bibliography of Related Reading
- Answer Key

We are confident that this unit will be a valuable addition to your planning, and we hope that as you use our ideas, your students will increase the circle of "friends" they have in books!

Standards

A Guide for Using Loser *in the Classroom* meets one or more of the following language arts standards, which are used with permission from McREL. (Copyright 2007, McREL, Mid-continent Research for Education and Learning. Telephone: 303-337-0990. Website: *www.mcrel.org*)

- Uses the general skills and strategies of the reading process.
- Uses reading skills and strategies to understand and interpret a variety of literary texts.
- Uses the general skills and strategies of the writing process.
- Uses the stylistic and rhetorical aspects of writing.
- Uses grammatical and mechanical conventions in written compositions.
- Gathers and uses information for research purposes.
- Uses listening and speaking strategies for different purposes.

Sample Lesson Plans

Each of the lessons suggested below can take from one to several days to complete.

Lesson 1

- Introduce and complete some or all of the pre-reading activities. (page 5)
- Highlight some of the novel's themes. (page 6)
- Read about the author. (page 7)
- Introduce the vocabulary for Section I. (page 9)

Lesson 2

- Read Chapters 1–8. As you read, place the vocabulary words in the context of the story and discuss their meanings.
- Chose a vocabulary activity. (page 10)
- Make snickerdoodles. (page 12)
- Write a speech of first graders. (page 13)
- Do some multiplication. (page 14)
- Begin Readers' Response Journals. (page 15)
- Administer the Section I quiz. (page 11)
- Introduce the vocabulary list for Section II. (page 9)

Lesson 3

- Read Chapters 9–12. Place the vocabulary words in context and discuss their meanings.
- Choose a vocabulary activity. (page 10)
- Help younger students. (page 17)
- Consider the importance of perceptions. (page 18)
- Look at the science of laughter. (page 19)
- Think about different occupations. (page 20)
- Administer Section II quiz. (page 16)
- Introduce the vocabulary list for Section III (page 9)

Lesson 4

- Read Chapters 13–18. Place the vocabulary words in context and discuss their meanings.
- Choose a vocabulary activity. (page. 10)
- Create a vivid picture. (page 22)
- Recognize value of supportive parents. (page 23)

- Learn about similes. (page 24)
- Find out about being a good friend. (page 25)
- Administer Section III quiz. (page 21)
- Introduce the vocabulary list for Section IV. (page 9)

Lesson 5

- Read Chapters 19–23. Place the vocabulary words in context and discuss meanings.
- Choose a vocabulary activity. (page 10)
- Make a candle (page 27)
- Consider differences. (page 28)
- Enjoy relay races. (page 29)
- Learn to deal with disappointment. (page 30)
- Administer Section IV quiz. (page 26)
- Introduce the vocabulary list for Section V. (page 9)

Lesson 6

- Read Chapters 24–30. Place the vocabulary words in context and discus meanings.
- Choose a vocabulary activity. (page 10)
- Create a class quilt. (page 32)
- Share positive traits. (page 33)
- Start a kazoo band. (page 34)
- Consider past and future changes. (page 35)
- Administer Section V quiz. (page 31)

Lesson 7

- Fill in the Open Mind. (page 36)
- Discuss questions your students have about the novel. (page 37)
- Assign book report and research activity. (pages 38-39)
- Begin work on one or more culminating activities. (pages 40-42)

Lesson 8

- Administer a Unit Test. (pages 43–45)
- Provide a list of related reading for your students. (page 46)

Before the Book

Before you begin reading *Loser* with your students, complete some pre-reading activities to stimulate interest and enhance comprehension. Here are some activities that might work well for your class.

1. Predict what the story might be about just by hearing the title. (You might tell the students that the story shows a character in his first six years of school.)

2. Predict what the story might be about just by looking at the cover illustration.

3. Discuss other books by Jerry Spinelli that students may have heard about or read.

4. Answer the following questions.

   - Are you interested in

     * stories about children your own age?

     * stories with modern settings?

     * stories that show what situations a child lives through as he grows up?

     * stories that have both funny and sad occurrences?

     * stories that show a unique perspective on life?

   - How might a child deal with the teasing of other children?

   - If you had to choose: Is it better to have many close friends or the support of your parents?

   - How can a young person remain unique and special when the rest of his world is telling him to be the same as everyone else?

5. Work in groups to create a factual or fictional story about a child who is being pressured by his or her classmates to act a certain way.

6. Research unique or special people who took a different path than most people and became successful.

Characteristics of a 'Loser'

The themes of Jerry Spinelli's *Loser* are complex. Your students will need help in discovering what makes Donald Zinkoff a heroic character. He has no superhero scene, and doesn't see any reason to change his distinctive perspective on life. The essence of Donald is his unique character. He embodies many of the characteristics adults will see as triumphant. Children, however, will probably not see that this boy is worth emulating. Children have a strong need for acceptance and will usually conform in order to gain their peers' favorable view. The teacher will need to work at making Donald's peculiar attitude acceptable.

This novel lends itself to lessons of values clarification. Here's one you might try before beginning the novel.

Discuss what a role model is. You might talk about what makes a good leader. You could choose leaders on the local, national, or international level that people admire and ask your students why they think people admire them.

Ask your students the following and have them share their answers with one another and then the class.

1. What qualities do you think a positive role model should possess?

2. List some famous names on the board—perhaps, include some you have already discussed. List some characteristics, behaviors, and traits you admire about each person whose name is listed on the board. Examples: Anne Frank. Rosa Parks, Cesar Chavez, Nelson Mandela, Helen Keller, Albert Einstein, Mother Teresa, Mahatma Gandhi.

3. What characteristics do most of these people have in common? How have your parents and teachers talked about these characteristics?

4. Think about your own personal role model. How do you consider your role model to be a good role model?

5. With a partner discuss the following: Think about the popular students at your school. Do these kids ever show characteristics that you do not admire? Without naming anyone, write down these negative characteristics and reasons why you feel they are negative.

Hopefully, you can guide the work so your students will see that it takes a strong individual to remain positive and committed to his/her values even when some people with negative traits are being looked up to. As you are reading *Loser*, you will be able to refer to this lesson. This will be especially valuable for those students who might comment that Donald is indeed a loser since he won't act in a way that will make him a popular student.

About the Author

Jerry Spinelli was born in Morristown, Pennsylvania, on February 1, 1941, to Louis A. and Lorna Mae (Bigler) Spinelli. His father was a printer. Jerry Spinelli attended Gettysburg College and received his M.A. from Johns Hopkins University in 1964. He married Eileen Mesi (a writer) in 1977, and they have seven children, three girls and four boys.

About his earliest writing, Mr. Spinelli says, "When I was sixteen, my high school football team won a big game. That night I wrote a poem about it. The poem was published in the local newspaper, and right about then I stopped wanting to become a major league shortstop and started wanting to become a writer."

When he first tried writing novels, Spinelli wrote for adults, but nobody was interested in publishing those novels. In his thirties he married Eileen, who had a half-dozen children. Suddenly Spinelli was a father, six times over! He recalls a night soon after his marriage: "One of our angels snuck into the refrigerator and swiped the fried chicken that I was saving for lunch the next day. When I discovered the chicken was gone, I did what I had done after the big football victory: I wrote about it.

His first novel for children was *Space Station Seventh Grade* (1982). It didn't have much to do with his grown-up years. It was mainly about his childhood. He realized he had enough memories for a "schoolbag of books." In 1984 he published *Who Put That Hair in My Toothbrush?* And in 1985, *Night of the Whale* became available to the public. His most famous novel, *Maniac Magee,* was published in 1990 and won the Newbery Medal the next year. Other novels by Spinelli are *Stargirl*, *Wringer*, and *The Library Card. Loser* was published in 2002.

Spinelli says, "I saw that each of us, in our kidhoods, was a Huckleberry Finn . . .I saw that each kid is a population unto him or herself, and that a child's bedroom is as much a window to the universe as an orbiting telescope or a philosopher's study."

Quotations and information for this biographical sketch were taken from *Something About the Author,* edited by Anne Commire, *Contemporary Authors,* edited by James G. Lesnick and from the internet service, galenet.galegroup.com

Loser

By Jerry Spinelli

Harper Trophy (Harper Collins Publishers), 2002

Donald Zinkoff grows up as a happy child loved by his parents. Donald is different than most boys because he enjoys playing and does not care if he wins the game or contest. He loves school right from the start and comes early. Once he even came on a Saturday.

His first grade teacher, Miss Meeks, tells the class that they will have 2,160 days in school and to make the most of them. Donald never forgets that number and wants to enjoy every one of them. Even though Miss Meeks is upset by Donald's penmanship and constant laughter, she is won over by his never-ending enthusiasm. Outside of school, Donald wins the championship game for his soccer team, even though it is a fluke.

Donald doesn't seem to mind that his second grade teacher, Mrs. Biswell, has a very difficult time dealing with his zest for life. He has one of his most valuable experiences when Mrs. Biswell insists on participation in Take Your Kid to Work Day. Donald's dad is a mailman and Donald can't wait to go on rounds with him. Donald is thrilled to deliver his scribbled letters to 100 houses and one dentist's office. On the route he sees the Waiting Man and the white-haired lady.

During third grade Donald must have an operation and stay home for several weeks. This is torture for him since Donald hates to have nothing to do. He gives himself a test to overcome his fear of the cellar and the noisy furnace. It is difficult for Donald, but he keeps trying until his fear gets the better of him.

The fourth grade is both wonderful and horrible for Donald. He has his favorite teacher, Mr. Yalowitz, who understands and appreciates Donald's individuality. For the first time, Donald gets to sit in the first row when Mr. Yalowitz announces that he seats by reverse alphabetical order. However, it is the year that students participate in Field Day, and Donald loses the competition for his team. It is the first time he hears the word 'Loser.'

In fifth grade, Donald tries to cultivate a best friend. It doesn't work out and his bad luck continues when no one wants him for their Field Day team. During graduation Donald slips on his way to receive his diploma, but his sister Polly saves the day by happily shouting out "Go Donald!"

In middle school, Donald refuses to be a "loser." When a little girl gets lost in a snowstorm, Donald searches for her for six hours. Calling on his positive attitude toward life, he refuses to give up. His family and neighbors congratulate him. It is Donald's individuality that makes him a very special boy.

Vocabulary Lists

On this page are vocabulary lists which correspond to each sectional grouping of chapters. Vocabulary activity ideas can be found on page 10 of this book.

Section I (Chapters 1–8)

trudge (trudging)	tintinnabulation
constraint	audible
headless	vigorous
giddy	legible
instinct	apparently
unpredictable	incredible
quiver	rekindle
atwitter	eruption(s)
equation	intrepid

Section II (Chapters 9–12)

haphazard	boondocks
slapdash	spatula
agape	harness(es)
slumped	expectation(s)
pedestal	triumph
atrocious	intrigue(d)
untimely	wispy
insulting	reluctant(ly)
intention	

Section III (Chapters 13–18)

convalesce(ing)	ponder(s)
immense	pronouncement(s)
twinge	stampede
flank	grimace(ing)
mock(ing)	invade (d)
congratulate	convenience
anchors	tote(ing)
clamber(s)	

Section IV (Chapters 19–23)

chaw	deliberate
petrified	transparent
ovation	astonish(ed
blunder(ing)	trounce(ing)
prominence	tantrum
veer(s)	hunker(s)
ultimate(ly)	pester(s)
woozy	

Section V (Chapters 24–30)

skirmish(es)	lurch(ing)
trample(d)	vast
ricochet(s)	hallucinate(ing)
loom(s)	
dislodge(d)	

Vocabulary Activity Ideas

You can help your students learn and retain the vocabulary in *Loser* by providing them with interesting vocabulary activities. Here are some ideas to try:

1. People of all ages like to make and solve puzzles. Ask your students to make their own **Crossword Puzzles** or **Word Search Puzzles** using the vocabulary words from the story.

2. Challenge your students to a **Vocabulary Bee!** This is similar to a spelling bee, but in addition to spelling each word correctly, the game participants must also correctly define each word.

3. Play **Vocabulary Concentration**. The goal in this game is to match vocabulary words with their definitions. Divide the class into groups of two to five students. Have students make two sets of cards the same size and color. On one set, have them write the vocabulary words. On the second set, have them write the definitions. All cards are mixed together and placed face down on a table. A player picks two cards. If the pair matches the word with its definition, the player keeps the cards and takes another turn. If the cards do not match, they are returned to their places face down on the table, and another player takes a turn. Players must concentrate to remember the locations of the words and their definitions. The game continues until all matches have been made. This is an ideal activity for free exploration time.

4. Have your students practice their writing skills by creating sentences and paragraphs in which multiple vocabulary words are used correctly. Ask them to share these **Compact Vocabulary sentences and paragraphs** with the class.

5. Ask your students to create paragraphs which use the vocabulary words to present **History Lessons** that relate to the time period of the novel.

6. Challenge your students to use a specific vocabulary word from the story at least ten times in one day. They must keep a record of when, how, and why the word was used!

7. As a group activity, have students work together to create an **Illustrated Dictionary** of the vocabulary words.

8. Play **20 Clues** with the entire class. In this game one student selects a vocabulary word and gives clues about this word, one by one, until someone in the class can guess the word.

9. Play **Vocabulary Charades**. In this game vocabulary words are acted out!

10. You probably have many more ideas to add to this list. Try them! See if experiencing vocabulary on a personal level increases your students' vocabulary interest and retention.

Quiz Time

Answer the following questions about Chapters 1–8.

1. Why does Mrs. Zinkoff return to her home with a "sigh of surrender" on Donald's first day of school?

   _____

   _____

2. Why is Mrs. Meeks worried about Donald?

   _____

   _____

3. Why is Donald placed in the very back of the classroom?

   _____

   _____

4. How does Donald surprise and upset the fourth grader who takes his hat?

   _____

   _____

5. How it is clear that Donald loves school?

   _____

   _____

6. When he is in first grade, how does Donald think his mother gets the shiny stars in her Baggie?

   _____

   _____

7. What deal does Mrs. Zinkoff make with Donald about the stars?

   _____

   _____

8. Why does Mrs. Meeks keep the "I Know I Can Behave" Button in her drawer instead of making Donald wear it?

   _____

   _____

9. Why doesn't Andrew want to come out of his room?

   _____

   _____

10. Besides the taste, what does Donald like about Snickerdoodles?

   _____

   _____

Snickerdoodles

In Chapter 8 of *Loser*, Donald bakes some cookies to make Andrew feel better. Donald chooses to make his favorites—Snickerdoodles. These cookies are pretty easy to make since there aren't many ingredients.

Some schools will have kitchen facilities so your class can make them together. But most of you will need to make them at home. Make sure you have an adult assist you. Yes, we know Donald wanted to make them all by himself, but his mother was close by in case he needed help.

There are many variations on the recipe for Snickerdoodles, but the one you'll find here is a classic. Recipes usually start with a list of ingredients, followed by how to combine them. Great cooks often put their own special touches on their meal. However, baking recipes must be followed carefully or they might not turn out the way you expect. Here it is—have fun!

Ingredients:

- ½ cup soft shortening
- ¾ cup sugar
- 1 egg
- 1 ⅓ cup sifted flour
- 1 teaspoon cream of tartar
- ½ teaspoon baking soda
- ⅛ teaspoon salt
- (later: 1 tablespoon sugar and 1 teaspoon cinnamon)

Directions:

1. Heat your oven to 400 degrees. Mix shortening, sugar, and egg thoroughly. Sift remaining ingredients together and stir into first mixture. Roll into balls the size of small walnuts.

2. Roll in mixture of the tablespoon of sugar and teaspoon of cinnamon. Place 2 inches apart on ungreased baking sheet. Bake 8 to 10 minutes until lightly browned but still soft. (They will puff up at first, then flatten out.) Cool; store in a covered jar or on a plate covered with tin foil.

3. This recipe will make approximately 2 ½ dozen 2-inch cookies. If you need more, you might want to make in two batches since doubling in the recipe can result in mistakes.

So you're thinking of making one large cookie like Donald did. This is not recommended since you know what happened to Donald's creation!!

A Speech to First Graders

In Chapter 5, Mrs. Meeks stands in front of Donald's class and welcomes them to the first grade. She calls them "young citizens" and welcomes them to climb aboard the learning train.

With a partner discuss answers to the following questions. After discussing, write down your collected answer to each of the following:

1. What is your opinion of the speech?

2. What do you feel is the best point that Mrs. Meeks makes to the students in her speech?

3. Mrs. Meeks mentions the word, "tintinnabulation." What are some of the funny sounding words that you know?

4. Locate the paragraph that begins "By the time you graduate from high school. . ." Do you think it is wise for young students to be thinking about their future? Why or why not?

5. Write down four or five ideas about what a student might say at beginning of the fourth or fifth grade.

On the lines below: Using your notes from questions 1–4, compose a speech that a student who has finished the fourth grade could say to the next class of fourth graders. Think about the things you learned and the projects you did.

_____

_____

_____

_____

_____

_____

_____

_____

Multiplication

Mrs. Meeks, in Chapter 5, astounds Donald by showing the class how many days they will be in school from grade 1–12. She multiplies the number of school days in each year (180) by the number of years (12) and the total is 2,160. Of course, the first graders have no idea what multiplication is, but you do. Set up the following problems (as Jerry Spinelli does in Chapter 5, and then find the answer.)

1. How old will you be on your next birthday? Figure out how many days you will have been alive on your next "big day."

   The number of days in a year x _____ (Age on my next birthday)

   Number of days I will have been alive _____

2. Figure out how many days one of your parents (or even a grandparent) has been alive.

   The number of days in a year   x _____ age of parent/grandparent

   Number of days they have been alive _____

3. Are you in school more days a year than you are off? Ask your teacher how many days are required in your district. Multiply by two.

   _____ x 2 = _____

   Is the answer higher or lower than 365? If it is lower than 365, you are off more days than you are in school. Were you surprised? _____

4. Approximately how many pages can you read in a week in a book you choose to read? _____ If you read that many pages every week for a year, how many pages would you read?

   Number of pages _____ x 52 (weeks in a year) = _____

Readers' Response Journals

One great way to ensure that reading Loser becomes a personal experience for each student is to include the use of Readers' Response Journals in your plans. In these journals, students can be encouraged to respond to the story in a number of ways. Here are a few ideas.

✐ Tell your students that the purpose of the journals is to record their thoughts, ideas, observations, and questions as they read *Loser*.

✐ Provide students with, or ask them to suggest, topics from the story that would stimulate writing. Here are a few examples from the chapters in Section I:

♣ How does the way people in your life act affect the way you feel towards life?

♣ Some readers might say that Donald has a positive attitude toward everything he does. What might this mean?

♣ By placing students in alphabetical order, the ones with the letters at the end always end up in the back. Why might this system by unfair?

✐ After the reading of each chapter, students can write one or more new things they learned in the chapter.

✐ Ask students to draw their responses to certain events or characters in the story, using blank pages in their journals.

✐ Tell students that they may use their journals to record "diary-type" responses that they may want to enter.

✐ Encourage student to bring their journal ideas to life! Ideas generated from their journal writing can be used to create plays, debates, stories, songs, and art displays.

✐ Give students quotes from the novel and ask them to write their own responses. Make sure to do this before you go over the quotations in class. In groups, they could list the different ways students respond to the same quote.

✐ Allow students time to write in their journals daily.

✐ Explain to the students that their Readers' Response Journals can be evaluated in a number of ways. Consider the following:

—Personal reflections will be read by the teacher, but no corrections or letter grades will be assigned. Credit is given for effort, and all students who sincerely try will be awarded credit. If a "grade" is desired for this type of entry, grade according to the number of journal entries completed. For example, if five journal assignments were made and the student conscientiously completes all five, then he or she receives an "A."

—Nonjudgmental teacher responses should be made as you read journals to let the students know you are reading and enjoying their journals. Here are some types of responses that will please your journal writers and encourage them to write more.

♣ "You have really found what's important in the story!"

♣ "You write so clearly. I almost feel as if I am there."

♣ "If you feel comfortable, I'd like to share this with the class. I think they'll enjoy it as much as I have."

Quiz Time

Answer the following questions about Chapters 9–12.

1. Why is soccer "Zinkoff's kind of game?" (How does it match Donald's personality?)

_____

_____

2. What is more important to Donald than winning the soccer game?

_____

_____

3. Several Titans want Donald traded to another team. Why are they glad that it didn't happen?

_____

_____

4. Andrew's team loses to Donald's team in the championship. What does Donald offer to do to make Andrew feel better?

_____

_____

5. How does Donald get on the wrong foot with his second-grade teacher almost immediately?

_____

_____

6. How does Donald "destroy" Mrs. Bidwell's eraser?

_____

_____

7. How does Mrs. Bidwell get into trouble with the principal?

_____

_____

8. Why must Donald go to "Take Your Kid to Work Day" on Sunday?

_____

_____

9. Donald's father uses the idiom, "piece of cake." What is he referring to?

_____

_____

10. What is "The Waiting Man" waiting for?

_____

_____

Helping Younger Students

In Chapter 10, Mrs. Bidwell asks Andrew to help Donald with his printing. Although Andrew isn't able to improve Donald's writing, it is a good idea for students to help their peers.

Another good idea is to have older students help younger ones. Since there are students in your school who need help with the basics of reading and writing, why not plan a class activity to assist their learning. Your students can assist the younger ones.

Contact a teacher in the first or second grade and suggest forming a cooperative learning group. Although the act of helping is worthwhile in itself, you might be looking for a way to use the experience as part of a specific project and as a way to fit into your standards. Here is an idea.

Making Students into Heroes

Your students will write a short story to create a storybook that uses the younger student as the main character. This activity will make both your students and the students they help into "heroes."

Steps to complete this project:

A. **Interviews**—prepare interview questions to determine the interests and dreams of the younger student.

B. **Short Story**—use what they learn about their student and compose a story that uses him or her as the central character—the hero of the story.

C. **Peer Reading**—your students help one another edit their stories.

D. **Technology**—After editing, your students can word process their story.

E. **Art**—create a picture (or series of pictures) to illustrate the story.

F. **Culminating Activity**—plan a special event where your students will share their work with the younger student. You can bet that this activity will make the younger students think that their older friend is a hero.

Extension Activities:

1. The younger students will want to keep the storybook forever. Before you give them away be sure to make a copy and bind them to keep for your future classes to see. (You will need to make a copy for your writers to keep too.)

2. If you take a few pictures during the interview, writing, and presentation parts, you will have the makings of a smashing bulletin board. Be sure to include examples of your students' work. Think how many standards can be highlighted.

3. Your colleague can have the younger students write thank-you notes to your students.

4. As the year progresses, the younger students might want to create a story about your students in a similar fashion.

Perceptions

One of Donald's most obvious characteristics is his positive attitude. It is Donald's view or perception of life that creates this attitude. Perhaps you've heard the famous saying by Abraham Lincoln, "People are just as happy as they make up their minds to be." Donald simply enjoys being happy. Andrew, Donald's next-door neighbor, seems to be much the opposite. His view or perception of life is negative.

With a partner discuss the following and decide on the best answer for the following questions about perceptions. Write your cooperative answers on the lines.

1. Donald really enjoys school. What are some of the ways the reader can see this?

   _____

   _____

2. Mrs. Bidwell's perception of school is negative. What are some of the ways you can tell?

   _____

   _____

   Finish the following statements showing how the situation can have a positive as well as a negative perception.

3. I am looking forward to the math test since

   _____

   _____

4. I am dreading the math test because

   _____

   _____

5. Our physical education program at this school is great since

   _____

   _____

6. Our physical education program at this school is horrible because

   _____

   _____

   Write the answer to these last two activities on another sheet of paper.

7. Compose a paragraph about the positive and negative aspects of the last novel your class read.

8. What conclusions can you make about positive and negative perceptions? Consider Abraham Lincoln's quote in your answer.

The Science of Laughter

Donald has a wonderfully positive outlook. He is almost always smiling and laughing. Did you know that there is scientific evidence that proves that laughing improves your body's well-being? Consider these three different levels:

1. Laughter improves the flow of oxygen to your organs. By the convulsive movements you have during laughing, oxygen moves around your body. This boosts your immune system and helps clear out old, dead waste products from organs and tissues. This movement helps to sustain life and fight off disease.

2. Laughter boosts our mental ability. The more oxygen flowing to your brain gives you a better ability to concentrate. All that laughing at recess can help with lessons when getting back to class.

3. Laughing is good exercise. Have you ever laughed so much that your stomach hurt? This is some serious exercise. This exhaustion has the same effect as a physical workout program.

Here's an hypothesis to consider: One scientific researcher said that every minute of laughter produces around $10,000 worth of healthy body chemicals! He says that there is a long list of chemicals created by laughter, including serotonin. If you tried to purchase these chemicals at a store they would cost you a fortune.

Now that we know some of benefits of laughing, the following two exercises could be worth even more than just having a great time.

1. Make a list of the things that typically make you laugh, especially when you are having a "bad" day. For the next two days create a list of the things that make you laugh.

2. For a journal topic, use your research on laughing to explain how enjoying a good laugh makes you feel better about

   a) getting out of bed on a school day

   b) doing chores around the house

   c) dealing with an upcoming test

   d) dealing with someone who has trouble understanding what you are explaining

Occupations

Donald's father is a postal carrier. We get a good idea of how Mr. Zinkoff's views his job when he takes Donald to "work" one Sunday. When we research occupations, we get a new understanding and appreciationof the work people do.

This activity will give you the opportunity to research an occupation of your choice.

I. Write down occupations of some people you know.

_____   _____

_____   _____

II. Which one of these occupations would you enjoy knowing more about? _____

III. Internet and/or research (locate answers to the following questions):

    a. What makes this occupation important to our society?

_____

_____

    b. How much education do you need to get this job?

_____

_____

    c. What is the common salary of this occupation?

_____

_____

    d. Is this an occupation that is easily done in your area, or where might you have to move to do it?

_____

_____

    e. Is this more of a physical or mental job? Explain.

_____

_____

    f. What are some of the interesting elements of this occupation?

_____

_____

    g. What are some of the drawbacks?

_____

_____

    h. Would you wish to find out more about this occupation for your future? Why?

_____

_____

IV. Report your findings to the class.

Quiz Time

Answer the following questions about Chapters 13–18.

1. Why must Donald go to the hospital? (What kind of operation does he have?)

   _____

   _____

2. Why does Donald's mother move Polly's playpen against the front door?

   _____

   _____

3. What is the one kind of darkness that Donald fears? Why?

   _____

   _____

4. At the end of Chapter 14, why does Donald think he has failed his own test?

   _____

   _____

5. Why do you think Mr. Yalowitz seats students in reverse alphabetical order?

   _____

   _____

6. What do "big-kid eyes" notice about Donald Zinkoff?

   _____

   _____

7. How does Donald lose the Field Day championship for the Purple Team?

   _____

   _____

8. How has Donald been "tagged and bagged" in the 5th grade?

   _____

   _____

9. What does Claudia's mother do to her daughter that surprises Donald?

   _____

   _____

10. Why does Donald choose Hector Binns as a best friend?

   _____

   _____

Representation: The Cellar

The longest sequence in the novel so far is when Donald tries to overcome his fear of the furnace in the dark and creepy cellar. If you reread this section in the chapter you see that Spinelli creates a vivid picture of Donald's experience. He makes us understand what is happening by appealing to three of our five senses—sight, sound, and touch. It is a scene that would work well in a movie.

Pretend you are an art director of a film and draw a picture of what you think a scene of the basement sequence would look like. Use the space below to make a rough drawing which you can later complete on another sheet of paper. You might consider a 3-dimensional representation. Can't you see the furnace in 3-D? Try to use some of the elements that Spinelli presents in words in your visual creation.

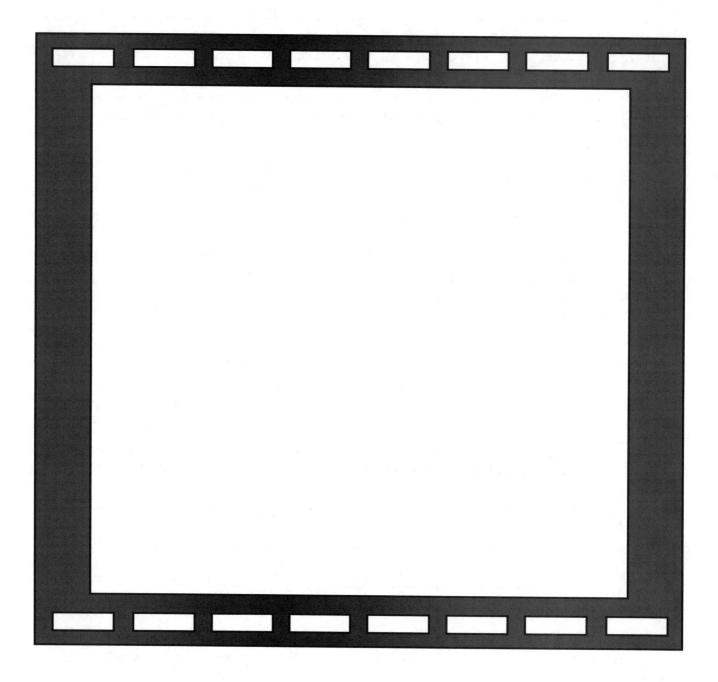

Supportive Parents

Donald has a mother and father who support his special abilities and positive outlook. He always knows, even after the horrible experience of Field Day that they will be there to help give him what he needs.

In this activity, work with a partner to answer the questions about *Loser* and then discuss and write down some of your thoughts about how parents can best support their children.

1. At the end of Chapter 16, how does Donald know that his dad will "never give up on him"?

_____

_____

_____

2. In chapter 17, how does Donald's mom show she respects his feelings when she is getting ready for the garage sale?

_____

_____

_____

3. As we get older, our parents support us in different ways than they did when we were first beginning school. What are some things that your parents used to help you with that you can now do on your own?

_____

_____

_____

4. What is a problem (or two) that a person in your grade would want to discuss with their parents? What kind of parental support would be most helpful with this particular problem?

_____

_____

_____

Animal Similes

In chapter 13, Spinelli writes this simile, "time sits on Zinkoff's hands like an elephant." This refers to how difficult it was for Donald to sit and wait, and it leads to his adventures in the dark and scary cellar.

A simile compares two things or objects that have little in common. To be a proper simile it must use "like" or "as" in its construction. A clever simile can bring a clear understanding to the situation. The heaviness of an elephant seems a perfect comparison to how difficult it is for Donald to wait.

Animal similes are common. In fact, there are few people who haven't heard that "she is as curious as a cat" or "he eats like a horse." Fill in the blanks below with the animal you think would be most commonly used for that simile. A list of the animals used are in the word box.

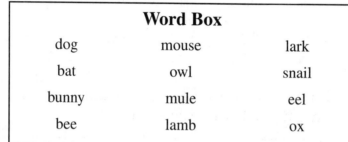

Word Box		
dog	mouse	lark
bat	owl	snail
bunny	mule	eel
bee	lamb	ox

1. You must speak up. You are as quiet as a _____.

2. I have a fever and want to go back to bed. I am as sick as a _____.

3. I couldn't grab the spoon. It was as slippery as an _____.

4. Ask George to help you lift the heavy box. He is as strong as an _____.

5. Alice beats everyone in the 50-yard dash. She's as quick as a _____.

6. Please don't bother me right now. I'm as busy as a _____.

7. The teacher will know the answer. He is as wise as an _____.

8. Wait until you go on the haunted house ride. You'll be as blind as a _____.

9. I've been waiting for the elevator for five minutes. It's as slow as a _____.

10. Don't worry about him. He is as gentle as a _____.

11. You'll never get your brother to change his mind. He's as stubborn as a _____.

12. She is always in such good spirits. I'd say she is as happy as a _____.

Being A Friend

In this section, Donald wants a best friend. He never has thought that much about it until he had to fill in blanks on a test. He chooses Hector Binns. Of course, we know a best friend is not chosen. Sometimes, creating a best friend is difficult. However, studies have shown there are some key elements that make good friendships work.

To have good friends you must be a good friend. Here are some of the ways good friends treat each other:

- Good friends listen to one another.

- Good friends don't put each other down or hurt each other's feelings.

- Good friends give each other compliments.

- Good friends are dependable and trustworthy.

- Good friends try to understand each other's feelings and moods.

- Good friends care about one another.

- Good friends listen to each other's problems and try to help solve them.

With a group of 3 or 4 students, discuss the following questions. Have one member of the group write down the ideas. Share them with the class.

1. Suppose you were invited to a birthday party of a class member, but your best friend who is also in the class was purposely left out. What would you do? Why?

   _____

   _____

   _____

2. Do best friends always have to do everything together? Do best friends always have to have the same friends?

   _____

   _____

   _____

3. We often hear that "To have good friends, you must be a good friend." What does this mean?

   _____

   _____

   _____

Quiz Time

Answer the following questions about Chapters 19–23.

1. Donald thinks best friends need to share. What does Donald share with Hector?

   _____

   _____

2. Why do you think the friendship between Donald and Hector does not work out?

   _____

   _____

3. Why does Donald receive his first ovation in school?

   _____

   _____

4. What does Donald realize when he hears the mail slot open at the old lady's house?

   _____

   _____

5. Why do you think Donald tells the old lady all about his life?

   _____

   _____

6. How does Donald see graduation from elementary school as a final test?

   _____

   _____

7. Why is Polly's reaction at graduation so important to Donald?

   _____

   _____

8. How does Andrew react when Donald calls to him on the first day of middle school?

   _____

   _____

9. What problem does Donald have in marching band?

   _____

   _____

10. What do you think Spinelli means when he says Donald "vanishes" in middle school?

    _____

    _____

Make A Candle

"Eewwwwww!" cries Polly when Donald tells the family that Hector Binns is planning to make a candle out of his own ear wax. However, with a bit of supervision, you can make a candle (out of paraffin wax, not ear wax!) that will make a welcome gift for someone in your family.

Milk Carton Candle

(Requires Supervision)

Materials

- small milk carton
- paraffin
- empty coffee can
- hot pads or mitts
- candle wicking or string
- saucepan
- craft stick

Put it Together!

1. Tie a length of wicking to the center of a craft stick.

2. Place some paraffin in a coffee can and place the can in a saucepan of boiling water to melt the paraffin.

3. Pour the melted paraffin into the milk carton. Be careful not to burn your hands on the hot coffee can. Use mitts or ask an adult to help you with this part.

4. Lower the wicking into the center of the paraffin, resting the craft stick on the top of the carton. Let the paraffin cool and harden and then clip the craft stick off, leaving a wick.

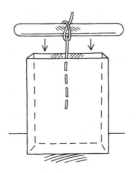

5. When wax has hardened, use a knife to cut around the sides of the carton to separate the wax from the carton.

Different?

Donald Zinkoff has found it difficult to make friends. People view him as different. Although he is loved at home, and his parents think he is just fine, at school he is an outsider. Even the teachers have trouble accepting Donald.

It is important to each of us to be accepted. We are concerned that others, especially those people our own age, see as "one of the group." In order to be accepted we must sometimes act in a way that is really not the way we feel or believe. When we consider it seriously, we know that it is the differences that make the world a more interesting place. Do we want a world where everyone acts the same? Do we want to live in a world where everyone looks the same? Differences enrich our lives.

In groups of three or four, list some of the differences you can find among those in your group. After you have completed your list, discuss how these differences make you and your classmates more interesting.

Here are some categories to help get the group started.

Physical Characteristics
- skin color
- eye color
- hair length and color
- height

Talents

Favorite school subjects

Family Size (numbers of brothers and sisters)

Birth Order

Favorite Possessions

Parents' Jobs

Hobbies

Fears

Favorite Foods

Sports Played

Have your group come up with four or five other categories and then list your differences for each one.

_____

_____

_____

_____

_____

_____

Relays

Donald Zinkoff practiced hard to be good at the Field Day relays. Relays are fun. Try some of the ones listed below. Perhaps your class will enjoy them so much that you want to plan your own Field Day.

- **Balloon Pop:** Provide each team with balloons—you'll need one per team member plus a couple of more, just in case. Inflate the balloons, so each is about the same size. Set up a chair for each team at a destination point. As the relay begins, the first member of the team carries a balloon to the chair, puts the balloon on the chair, and then sits on the balloon until it pops. When the balloon pops, the student runs back to his or her team and tags the next person in line. The relay continues until the last student in each team has made it back to the line. The first team to finish wins.

- **Suitcase Madness:** Provide each team with a suitcase of old clothes, containing a pair of oversized pants, an oversized shirt, and large shoes. (If you really want hysterical students, include colorful boxer shorts and an outrageous hat.) When the relay begins, the first member of each team runs to the destination spot with suitcase in hand, opens the suitcase, and puts on each of the clothing items over his or her own clothing. When that student is fully dressed, he or she undresses, packs up the suitcase, and runs back to the team. He or she then hands off the suitcase to the next student and the relay continues… The relay ends when the last student returns to the team with the packed-up suitcase. The team that finishes fastest wins. (You might have each pose while dressed while a photo is taken.)

- **Orange You Having Fun??** Teams stand in a line with the first member of the team holding an orange (or other similar-sized fruit.) The objective is to pass the orange down the line to the last team member without using their hands. This is done by gripping the orange under your chin (remember, no hands!), then turning around to face the next person and for them to take the orange from you by gripping it under their chin. This process is repeated down the line to the last person. Either stop the relay at this point or have the last person run to the front and start again. The race stops when the first person ends up at the front again. If you drop the orange while passing it, you must start over with the first person!

- **Don't Egg Us On!** Each player has to run balancing an egg (raw or hard boiled) on a spoon. (Or, if you prefer, use marbles.) If the object falls off the spoon, players have to stop, pick it up and replace it before running on again to a destination point and back to the next in line.

- **Mummy!!** You'll need plenty of economy toilet-paper rolls. One team member is nominated to stand perfectly still. Other team members then have to wrap him or her up so they look like an Egyptian mummy. Points awarded for first to finish and points to best-dressed mummy.

  Try this variation and have teams of 6. Each member wraps one body part: arm (2), leg (2), head—there should be only one of those!

Dealing with Disappointment

Donald is learning to deal with disappointment in his life. He has been a happy child, but now it is important for him to feel more accepted by his peers. Each of us must learn how to cope when life isn't what we wish it to be. Here are some ways of keeping disappointment from getting you down.

- Don't feel that you have failed. Having a disappointment doesn't mean that you are a failure.

- Ask yourself if this situation is really worth getting so angry or upset about.

- Don't make any hasty decisions. Give yourself some time and space. The situation may not seem so horrible tomorrow.

- Talk about the situation with your parents, teacher, or a good friend.

- Think about how you could learn from this experience and how you might do better the next time.

Here are some activities you can do to help you learn how to deal with disappointment:

1. Ask a family member or an adult you respect to tell you about a situation when he or she felt disappointed because something didn't turn out the way they wished it had. How did he or she deal with the disappointment? How might they have handled it differently? (You might write this in a question and answer form.)

    _____

    _____

    _____

2. Do you have a favorite story or movie where the main character must deal with a problem? If you think about it, almost all stories are about solving a problem. What novels have you read beside *Loser* that are about a boy or girl who must deal with disappointment? Write a report about one novel or movie, focusing on the problem that a character has. How does he or she deal with this problem? Is the outcome positive or negative? What can a person who reads this novel (or watches the movie) learn from it?

    _____

    _____

    _____

3. Look in the newspaper, magazines, or online for stories of people who have dealt with disappointment and have had positive outcomes. Cut out (or download) the stories and place them in a folder. As you read each story consider what kind of thinking the person had to go through to solve the problem or make the situation better. Write down what you have learned from each article.

    _____

    _____

    _____

Quiz Time

Answer the following questions about Chapters 24–30.

1. Why are there police cars and emergency vehicles on Willow Street?

    _____

    _____

2. Why do you think Donald pulls out his lucky stone and "clutches" it in his hand?

    _____

    _____

3. As he is looking for Claudia, why does Donald think of his sister Polly?

    _____

    _____

4. Donald wants to stop looking and go home to get warm. Why do you think he doesn't?

    _____

    _____

5. If Claudia isn't found, what does Donald imagine will happen to her mother?

    _____

    _____

6. Write down three of the experiences Donald has while looking for Claudia.

    _____

    _____

7. What time was Donald found? What time was Claudia found?

    _____

    _____

8. Why do you think Claudia's mother holds Donald and "won't let him go?"

    _____

    _____

9. It wasn't the police that found Donald. Who was it?

    _____

    _____

10. Why do you think Bonce calls out "Zinkoff" and lets him join his team?

    _____

    _____

Creating a Class Quilt

At the end of the novel there is an interesting scene where Bonce picks Donald to be on his football team. At first, the boys make fun of Donald. However, Donald refuses to leave, and eventually Bonce calls his name. The events of the previous days—looking for Claudia and everyone coming to see him—has made Donald feel good about himself again. We again see all the special qualities that make Donald the unique person he is.

You also have many abilities and interests that make you the special person you are. Each person in your class is special in his or her own way.

To celebrate these qualities, you can create a class quilt. Each member will have a square that will reveal his or her individuality.

Create a Class Quilt

Materials:

- 8 ½ inch (22 cm) squares of white paper - one for each student

- 10-inch (25 cm) square pieces of construction paper, various colors

- magazines, scissors, and glue

- markers, crayons, and other art supplies

- a roll of wide masking tape

Each student gets a piece of white paper on which to create an art work that shows his or her interests, thoughts, future plans, or whatever he or she wants. Students can use art supplies or create a collage by cutting pictures out of magazines.

After the students have completed their artwork, have each select a piece of construction paper. Ask them to glue their artwork in the middle so the construction paper creates a frame around each piece.

After the class is finished, use wide masking tape to create the quilt. Turn over the square pieces of construction paper and lay them in the pattern you wish on the floor. Using the tape to fasten the pieces together, you will create a beautiful class quilt.

Two poems you can use with this quilt activity are "My Mother Pieced Quilts" by Teresa Palomo Acosta and "Quilt" by John Updike.

Sharing Circles

Positive Traits:

In *Loser*, Jerry Spinelli wants the reader to consider how each of us is different and that those differences are what make us unique. Donald may not be like most of the others in his class, but he should be recognized for his special qualities.

To the Teacher: In these exercises, students will be able to recognize positive traits in themselves and others and develop a habit of talking about positive traits.

Discuss the concept of a positive or negative atmosphere in the classroom and how it affects how we feel about each other. A negative atmosphere is created when students and teachers use put-downs, pointing out only negatives qualities. A positive atmosphere is created when we look for and talk about the good qualities. Create this positive atmosphere by practicing 'put-ups!'

Procedure:

1. Use this daily exercise for 10 to 15 minutes for a week or more.
2. Seat students in a circle facing each other.
3. Explain "Sharing Circle" rules as follows:

    Students take turns, going around the circle until everyone has spoken. One person speaks at a time.

    No interruptions, laughing at, or comments allowed.

    Listen to the person who is speaking.

    When it is your turn, share one brief answer on the topic given.
4. Write the topic on the chalkboard, say it loud, then allow a minute or more for your students to think before beginning the circle.

Topics:

Day 1: "Something that I like in other people is…" (Suggested examples: "I like people who are honest." I like people who listen to me.")

Day 2: "Something I like in myself is…" (Examples: "I like that I'm smart. I can keep a secret")

Day 3: "Something I like or appreciate about the person to my right is… " (Examples: She is funny. He is friendly. He draws pictures for me." Emphasize that all comments must be 'put-ups.')

Day 4 and on: "Who can remember a time when (supply student's name) did something very special and caring for someone in class? (You can begin by filling in an example about one of your students. Encourage students to relate the special deeds children have done in class or on the playground.)

You might want to have each student name a positive characteristic that his or her example shows:

Courage	*Enthusiasm*	*Strength (of character)*
Joy	*Understanding*	*Caring*
Trust	*Honesty*	*Support*

Display these appreciations in the classroom. You might want to create a tree where each leaf is one of the 'put-ups.' You'll certainly want to be sure that every student in the classroom is represented.

Form a Kazoo Band!

Although Donald had trouble marching and playing his flute at the same time, he loved being in the band. Have you ever tried forming a kazoo band? It doesn't take much preparation yet you can give your students lessons in cooperating, learning about famous march music, and you'll all have a great time.

Making a Kazoo

Although a kazoo doesn't cost very much to buy, it is fun to make. After decorating them, each student will have a unique 'instrument.' (And isn't uniqueness what *Loser* is all about?)

Materials:

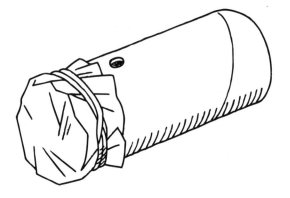

- Cardboard tube (e.g. toilet-paper roll)
- Wax paper (or tissue)
- Hole punch
- Construction Paper
- Scissors
- Crayons, markers or paint and brushes
- Tape or glue (or rubber bands)

1. Punch a hole in the toilet-paper roll, as far in as the hole punch will reach.

2. Cut a circle out of wax paper about 1" larger in diameter than the tube. Glue, tape or rubber band the waxed paper over one end of the tube. Do not cover the hole. The waxed paper needs to be taut with only a bit of play.

3. Decorate.

4. To play, hum into the open end of the roll. Your breath makes the wax paper vibrate. The hole lets the air escape.

Now it's time to get the band working together.

1. Find some appropriate march music. This could be a great time to teach some patriotic music. If you can find a CD it will be much easier to teach.

2. Now it's time to try some movement.

   a. Line students up and practice marching on the playground. Nothing fancy at first. Just make sure they know their left foot from their right. Everyone starts on left.

   b. After they get the hang of it, try it with the kazoos. It may sound easy but some of your students will probably feel a bit of the frustration Donald felt.

   c. The rest is all about how adventurous you want to be. You can divide your class into four groups and have them march in formation. Once they can do it with straight lines try some more intricate patterns. They will have a great time and learn something about rhythm and teamwork too.

Changes

In this story, Donald goes through many changes. We also go through changes as we go through our lives. Think about what you are like now. How have you changed since you were a young child? What will you be like when you graduate from high school? What will you be like ten years after graduating from high school? Use the spaces below to show yourself at four different stages of life. Then, on the back of this paper, write a paragraph telling about some of your goals for the future.

ME (as a young child)	**ME (as I am right now)**
ME (when I graduate from high school)	**ME (ten years after graduating)**

Open Mind

Many thoughts and images run through our minds at almost any moment. There are things we choose to think about and others that are involuntary. A well-written fictional character comes alive to us in the ways he or she think, (as well as act). Choose an important incident in *Loser* and consider it from Donald's point of view. Inside the silhouette below, visually represent Donald's thoughts through words and/or pictures.

The incident: _____

_____

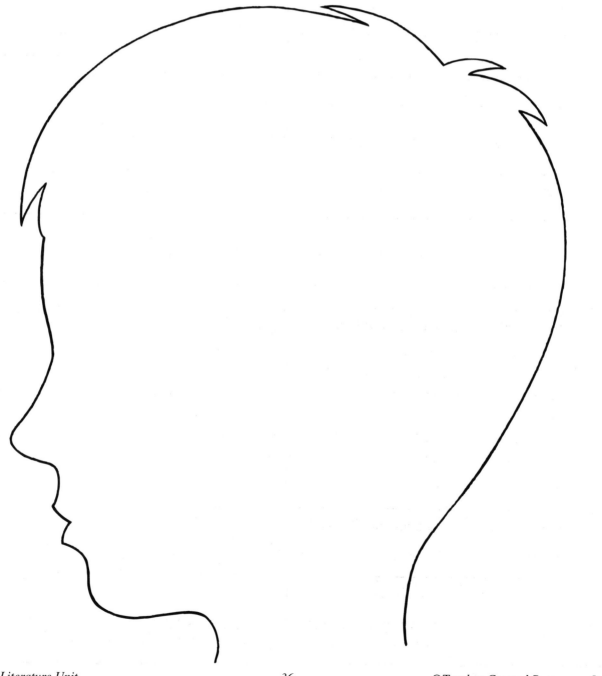

Any Questions?

When you finished reading *Loser*, you probably had some questions that were left unanswered. Write them on the back of this page. Then work in groups or by yourself to prepare possible answers for the questions you have asked or for those written below. When you have finished, share your ideas with the class.

1. Does the Waiting Man ever stop waiting for his brother to return from Vietnam? Why or why not?_____

_____

2. Do the Waiting Man and Donald ever have a conversation? If so, what do they talk about?

_____

_____

3. Does Donald continue to see Claudia and her mother? _____

_____

4. Do Donald and Hector Binns see each other in middle school? Do they become friends?

_____

_____

5. Does Donald ever have a best friend? What is he or she like? _____

_____

6. What interests does Donald develop in high school?

_____

_____

7. Does Donald ever learn to march and play the flute at the same time? Why or why not?

_____

_____

8. Does Donald ever go back and see Mr. Yalowitz? Why or why not?

_____

_____

9. Does Donald remember the number 2,160 on the day he graduates from high school? How does he react? _____

_____

10. When is Donald able to go down into the cellar and not be afraid?

_____

_____

11. Does Donald become a mailman like his father? Why or why not?

_____

_____

12. If he doesn't become a mailman, what occupation does Donald have?

_____

_____

Book Report Ideas

There are numerous ways to report on a book once you have read it. After you have finished reading *Loser*, choose one method of reporting on the book that interests you. It may be a way your teacher suggests, and idea of your own, or one of the ways that is mentioned below.

See What I Read?

This report is a visual one. A model of a scene from the story can be created, or a likeness of one or more of the characters from the story can be drawn or sculpted.

Time Capsule

This report provides people living at a future time with the reasons *Loser* is such an outstanding book. Make a time capsule and neatly print or write your reasons inside the capsule. You may wish to "bury" your capsule after you have shared it with your classmates. Perhaps one day someone will find it and read *Loser* because of what you wrote!

Come to Life!

This report is one that lends itself to a group project. A size-appropriate group prepares a scene from the story for dramatization, acts it out, and relates the significance of the scene to the entire book. Costumes and props will add to the dramatization!

Into the Future

This report predicts what might happen if *Loser* were to continue. It may take the form of a story in narrative or dramatic form, or it may be a visual display.

Guess Who or What

This report is similar to "Twenty Questions." The reporter gives a series of clues about a character from the story in vague-to-precise, general-to-specific order. After all clues have been given, the identity of the mystery character must be deduced. After the character has been guessed, the same reporter presents another "Twenty Questions" about an event in the story.

Sales Talk

This report serves as an advertisement to "sell" *Loser* to one or more specific groups. You decide on the group to target and the pitch you will use. Include some kind of graphics or visual aid in your presentation.

Literary Interview

This report is done in pairs. One student will pretend to be a character in the story. The student will play the role of a television or radio interviewer, trying to provide the audience with insights into the character's personality and life. It is the responsibility of the partners to create meaningful questions and appropriate responses.

Research Late Bloomers

Donald Zinkoff has many fine qualities. His uniqueness has caused him problems in school. Many famous people who seemed different when they were young became famous in their later years. A late bloomer is a person who does not discover his or her talents and abilities until later than normally expected. In certain cases, the individual may have been as old as 60. Research one of the following famous late bloomers.

Art
- Grandma Moses began her painting career when she was in her seventies.
- Bill Traylor started drawing at age 83.
- Alfred Wallis began painting after his wife's death in his sixties.

Business
- Colonel Sanders (Harlan) began his famous Kentucky Fried Chicken franchise in his sixties.
- Taikichiro Mori founded a business that once made him the richest man in the world. He was over 50.
- Ray Kroc started franchising McDonald's in his fifties.
- Armand Hammer was a millionaire many times over but really began when he bought Occidental Petroleum when he was almost 60.

Sports
- Joshua Milner was 61 when he won his Olympic gold medal.
- Oscar Swahn won Olympic medals at 60 and 72.
- Philip Rabinowitz set a sprinting record for centenarians. (You know how long a century is!)
- Kurt Warner entered the NFL at 28.
- Randy Johnson didn't become a superstar baseball pitcher until he was 30.
- Cliff Young won an Australian Marathon at 61.
- Francis Chichester sailed around the world in a yacht at 65, the first person ever to do it solo.

Music
- Anton Bruckner didn't become a classical composer until his forties.
- Singer K.T. Oslin released her first album at 47.
- Singer Al Jarreau released his first album at 38.

Writing
- Mary Wesley wrote two children's book in her late fifties, and her first novel at 70.
- Harriet Doerr published her first novel at 74.
- Laura Ingalls Wilder didn't publish *Little House on the Prairie* until her sixties.
- Richard Adams published *Watership Down* when in his fifties.
- Raymond Chandler published his first short story at 45.
- Novelist Edith Wharton wrote 40 books but didn't publish the first one until she was 43.

Medicine
- The Nobel Laureate, Albert Schweitzer, didn't study medicine until he was 38.

Politics
- Lech Walesa was president of Poland but he didn't even consider running for office until he was 37.
- Ronald Reagan didn't enter politics until he was in his thirties.

The Bells

One of Donald's favorite words is TINTINNABULATION. He heard it on the first day of first grade and never forgot it. The word is used the marvelous poem, *The Bells* by Edgar Allan Poe. It is toward the end of the first stanza.

Here's something you can use as a choral reading for your class. There are so many wonderful new words to learn, and when they understand the use of rhythms they will keep them the rest of their lives. And, of course, they, too, will never forget TINTINNABULATION!!

Here are some ideas to use in your choral reading.

1. The poem is divided into four stanzas, each celebrating a different size bell: sleigh bells, wedding bells, alarm bells, funeral bells. Divide your class into four sections.

2. The constant repetition of the word 'bells' is to simulate the back and forth movement of the clapper inside the bells. Without that movement there would be no sound. Have the whole class join in on the word "bells."

3. Each successive bell has a lower sound. You might have the higher voices on the first two stanzas and the lower voices on the last two. Having students learn to speak together so they can be heard is time consuming. You probably will want to divide the lines so that each student has two or three. The meaning in the lines divide easily into two or three line segments. Example of the first stanza:

Hear the sledges with the bells
Silver bells!
What a world of merriment their melody foretells!

How they tinkle, tinkle, tinkle,
In the icy air of night!

While the stars that over sprinkle
All the heavens, seem to twinkle
With a crystalline delight;

Keeping time, time, time,
In a sort of Runic rhyme,
To the tintinnabulation that so musically wells

(these lines the class does together)
From the bells, bells, bells, bells,
Bells, bells, bells,
From the jingling and the tinkling of the bells

4. It is a choral reading, not a memorization exercise. Some of your students will, undoubtedly memorize, but unless you have an especially adept class, don't make this a requirement. The idea is to work together to create an effect. Memorization will get in the way of a finished product. Give each student his or her own copy of the poem to use while practicing and in performance.

5. Find a recording of the poem to play for your class. This will help them get the words and rhythms. One can be found at *www. reelyredd.com*.

6. Ask the music teacher if he or she would like to make this a joint effort.

7. There are so many ways you can teach poetry through this poem. One of the figures of language used is onomatopoeia (which your students will also love to say). Have them find those imitating-the-sound-they-make words like *jingling, tinkling, clang, clash, roar* and explain how they add to the poem's effect. Then have them find onomatopoeic words in their own life.

8. Perform for other classes and parents. Have fun!!

The Bells
by
Edgar Allan Poe

I

Hear the sledges with the bells -
Silver bells!
What a world of merriment their
melody foretells!
How they tinkle, tinkle, tinkle,
In the icy air of night!
While the stars that oversprinkle
All the heavens seem to twinkle
With a crystalline delight;
Keeping time, time, time,
In a sort of Runic rhyme,
To the tintinnabulation that so
musically wells
From the bells, bells, bells, bells,
Bells, bells, bells -
From the jingling and the tinkling of
the bells.

II

Hear the mellow wedding bells -
Golden bells!
What a world of happiness their
harmony foretells!
Through the balmy air of night
How they ring out their delight!
From the molten-golden notes,
And all in tune,
What a liquid ditty floats
To the turtle-dove that listens, while
she gloats
On the moon!
Oh, from out the sounding cells
What a gush of euphony voluminously
wells!
How it swells!
How it dwells
On the Future! -how it tells
Of the rapture that impels
To the swinging and the ringing
Of the bells, bells, bells,
Of the bells, bells, bells, bells,
Bells, bells, bells -
To the rhyming and the chiming of the
bells!

III

Hear the loud alarum bells -
Brazen bells!
What a tale of terror, now, their
turbulency tells!
In the startled ear of night
How they scream out their affright!
Too much horrified to speak,
They can only shriek, shriek,
Out of tune,
In a clamorous appealing to the mercy
of the fire,
In a mad expostulation with the deaf
and frantic fire,
Leaping higher, higher, higher,
With a desperate desire,
And a resolute endeavor
Now -now to sit or never,
By the side of the pale-faced moon.
Oh, the bells, bells, bells!
What a tale their terror tells
Of despair!
How they clang, and clash, and roar!
What a horror they outpour
On the bosom of the palpitating air!
Yet the ear it fully knows,
By the twanging
And the clanging,
How the danger ebbs and flows;
Yet the ear distinctly tells,
In the jangling
And the wrangling,
How the danger sinks and swells,
By the sinking or the swelling in the
anger of the bells -
Of the bells,
Of the bells, bells, bells, bells,
Bells, bells, bells -
In the clamor and the clangor of the
bells!

IV

Hear the tolling of the bells -
Iron bells!
What a world of solemn thought their
monody compels!

In the silence of the night,
How we shiver with affright
At the melancholy menace of their
tone!
For every sound that floats
From the rust within their throats
Is a groan.
And the people -ah, the people -
They that dwell up in the steeple,
All alone,
And who tolling, tolling, tolling,
In that muffled monotone,
Feel a glory in so rolling
On the human heart a stone -
They are neither man nor woman -
They are neither brute nor human -
They are Ghouls:
And their king it is who tolls;
And he rolls, rolls, rolls,
Rolls
A paean from the bells!
And his merry bosom swells
With the paean of the bells!
And he dances, and he yells;
Keeping time, time, time,
In a sort of Runic rhyme,
To the paean of the bells,
Of the bells -
Keeping time, time, time,
In a sort of Runic rhyme,
To the throbbing of the bells,
Of the bells, bells, bells -
To the sobbing of the bells;
Keeping time, time, time,
As he knells, knells, knells,
In a happy Runic rhyme,
To the rolling of the bells,
Of the bells, bells, bells -
To the tolling of the bells,
Of the bells, bells, bells, bells,
Bells, bells, bells -
To the moaning and the groaning of the
bells.

Connections

At the end of Chapter 27, Donald starts to hallucinate because of the cold and his exhaustion. He starts thinking and talking about his past. For each of the following, connect to the moment in the novel when he first heard each of them.

"piece of cake"

"TINTINNABULATION"

"Go Donald!"

"AND THE Z SHALL BE FIRST"

"yellow button"

"Get off my team"

"One thousand congratulations"

"Jabip"

"Good morning young citizens"

"Heaven help (me)"

Unit Test

Matching: Match the quote with the person who said it.

a. Donald   e. Mr. Zinkoff

b. Andrew   f. Mrs. Zinkoff

c. Mrs. Biswell   g. Hector Binns

d. Mr. Yalowitz   h. Gary Hobin

1. _____ "Okay. Enough of this chitchat. Time to hit the trail. Let's go. People are waiting for their mail."

2. _____ "We could make a deal. We could wait until you're having a really bad day, some day when you could really, really use two stars to pick you up. That's when you get them."

3. _____ "His name's Zinkoff. He went to my school. He's nobody."

4. _____ "Out! Out! Out! Get out of my classroom and never come back!"

5. _____ "What I think is, when I get enough wax I'm gonna make a candle."

6. _____ "We're eating lunch in a restaurant. Sometimes the mayor goes there. My dad says when he gets a raise, we're outta here. He says we're never coming back to this dump."

7. _____ "And the Z shall be first!"

8. _____ "My lucky stone!. . . Mom, drop it! You can't touch it. . . Nobody can touch it but me."

True or False: Write true or false next to each statement below.

1. Donald would rather be in school than at home.
2. Mr. Zinkoff often tells Donald he must act like other children.
3. Hector Binns is enthusiastic when Donald tells him they should be friends.
4. Donald overcomes his fear of the furnace and the dark cellar.
5. Donald finds Claudia in an alley partially covered with snow.

Sequence: Put these events in order by number (1 to 5) on the lines.

_____ Donald goes to work with his dad.

_____ Donald brings Andrew a giant-sized Snickerdoodle.

_____ Relatives and neighbors come to congratulate Donald.

_____ A teacher tells Donald about how many days he will go to school.

_____ Donald skips school on Field Day.

Paragraphs: Answer the following in paragraph form on the back of this sheet.

1. What is a characteristic of Donald's personality that makes him want to find Claudia? Use examples of this characteristic you have seen earlier in the novel.

2. Reread the last paragraph of chapter 16. Explain how Donald feels after talking to his dad on the day of the fourth-grade field day.

Responding to Quotes

On a separate piece of paper, explain a possible meaning of each of these quotations from *Loser*. Try to find a unique meaning "behind' the words.

Chapter 1: "You grow up with a kid but you never really notice him."

Chapter 3: "Burping, growing, throwing, running—everything is a race."

Chapter 5: "What a wonderful adventure it will be!"

Chapter 6: "Even when you yourself are not in a particular place, your name can be there."

Chapter 7: "He keeps erupting through dinner. Eating becomes hazardous."

Chapter 8: "Early on, Zinkoff's mother impressed upon her son the etiquette of throwing up."

Chapter 9: "Zinkoff is determined to become a better loser."

Chapter 10: "It is the Rolls Royce of greenboard erasers."

Chapter 13: "His world shrinks to the living-room sofa."

Chapter 14: "A smear of light puddles at the far corner of the furnace."

Chapter 15: "Big-kid eyes are picky."

Chapter 16: "He knows that if he ever springs a leak or throws a gasket, his dad will be there with duct tape and chewing gum to patch him up, that no matter how much he rattles and knocks, he'll always be a honeybug to his dad, never a clunker."

Chapter 18: "His eyes have gone back to the Beyond."

Chapter 20: "The town is the same and not the same."

Chapter 21: "Like stones, he drops each sound into those uncrying eyes."

Chapter 22: "Boondocks forever."

Chapter 23: "Long before the first snowfall, he sinks into nobodyness."

Chapter 25: "The light from the nearest streetlamp follows him, loses him."

Chapter 26: "He wonders if angels are invisible in the snow. He wonders if angels make people in the snow."

Chapter 28: "She (Claudia's mother) just sits on the sofa and pulls him into herself and won't let him go."

Chapter 30: ". . . but in the end there's really only one word, he (Bonce) knows that, one word from him and who knows where we go from there?"

Conversations

Work in size-appropriate groups to write and perform the conversations that might have occurred in the following situations. If you prefer, you may use your own conversation idea for characters from *Loser*.

* Mr. and Mrs. Zinkoff have a talk about Donald the day before he begins first grade. (2 people)

* Mrs. Bidwell tells her husband about Donald after the first day of second grade. (2 people)

* The principal and Mrs. Bidwell discuss the situation after he finds out she sent Donald home. (2 people)

* Andrew and his mother argue when he walks into the house with Donald's trophy. (2 people)

* Donald tells Mr. Yalowitz what it means to sit in the front of the classroom. (2 people)

* Donald and his dad discuss what happened at the fourth grade Field Day. (2 people)

* Donald and Claudia's mother have a longer discussion about the value of the leash. (2 people)

* Hector Binns gives details to Donald about how he will make his ear-wax candle. (2 people)

* Mr. and Mrs. Zinkoff, Donald, and Polly chat about the graduation ceremony on the way home in the car. (4 people)

* Donald and Mr. and Mrs. Zinkoff talk in detail about what happened to Donald while he was looking for Claudia. (3 people)

* Donald and Claudia's mother have a talk when she comes to see him after his experience in the snow. (2 people)

In the future:

* Donald goes back to see Mr. Yalowitz to get some ideas about how to handle middle school. (2 people)

* In high school, Andrew and Donald have a class together. They begin to be friendly. What might they talk about? (2 people)

* Mr. and Mrs. Zinkoff and Donald have a discussion the day of Donald's high school graduation. (3 people)

Bibliography of Related Reading

Fiction—Contemporary Life and Problems

Abbot, Tony. *Firegirl*. (Little Brow, 2006)

Avi. *Crispin: The Cross of Lead*. (Hyperion, 2002)

Bradby, Marie. *Some Friend*. (Atheneum, 2004)

Choldenko, Gennifer. *Al Capone Does My Shirts*. (Puffin, 2006)

Creech, Sharon. *Heartbeat*. (Joanna Colter, 2004)

---*Walk Two Moons*. (HarperTrophy, 1996)

Crutcher, Chris. *Staying Fat for Sarah Byrnes*. (Greenwillow, 1993)

DiCamillo, Kate. *Because of Winn-Dixie*. (Candlewick, 2000)

Dowell, Frances O'Roark. *Chicken Boy*. (Antheneum, 2005)

Going, K.L. *the Liberation of Gabriel King*. (Putnam, 2005)

Henkes, Kevin. *Olive's Ocean*. (Greenwillow, 2003)

Kadohata, Cynthia. *Kira-Kira*. (Antheneum, 2004)

Lowry, Lois. *The Giver*. (Walter Lorraine, 1993)

Paulsen, Gary. *Harris and Me: A Summer Remembered*. (Harcourt, 1993)

Sacher, Louis. *Holes*. (Foster, 1998)

Spinelli, Jerry. *Maniac Magee*. (HarperTrophy, 1990)

---*Stargirl*. (Knopf, 2000)

---*Wringer*. (Joanna Colter, 1997)

Tasjian, Janet. *The Gospel According to Larry*. (Henry Holt, 2001)

Nonfiction

Beckham, David. *David Beckham's Soccer Skills*. (HarperCollins, 2007)

Booher, Dianna. *Making Friends with Yourself & Other Strangers*. (Messner, 1982)

Crisfield, Deborah W. *The Everything Kids' Soccer Book*. (Adams Media, 2002)

Crisswell, Patti Kelly. *A Smart Girl's Guide to Friendship Troubles*. (American Girl, 2003)

Cohen, Susan and Donald Cohen. *Teenage Stress*. (Evans, 1984)

Herron, Ronald W. *A Good Friend: How to Make One, How to Be One*. (Boys Town Press, 1998)

Kennedy, Rod. *Monopoly: The Story Behind the World's Best Selling Game*. (MJF, 2006)

Orbanes, Philip. *The Monopoly Companion: the Player's Guide*. (Sterling, 2007)

Varenhorst, Barbara. *Real Friends: Becoming the Friend You'd Like to Have*. (Harper, 1983)

Ward, Hiley. *Feeling Good About Myself*. (Westminster, 1983)

For Teachers:

Cook, Mark. *Levels of Personality*. (Continuum Press, 1993)

Danzig, Robert J. *There is Only One You: You Are Unique in the Universe*. (Child Welfare League of America, 2003)

Harris, Judith. *No Two Alike: Human Nature and Human Individuality*. (Norton, 2006)

Lerner, Stephanie. *Kids Who Think Outside the Box*. (AMACOM, 2005)

Thomas, Alexander. *Behavioral Individuality in Early Childhood*. (Greenwood, 1980)

Tobias. Cynthia Ulrich. *The Way They Learn*. (Tyndale House, 1998)

Answer Key

Page 11

1. Donald does not wait for Mrs. Zinkoff to take him to school on the first day.

2. Mrs. Meeks sees Donald's giraffe hat and wonders if he is going to be a troublemaker.

3. Mrs. Meeks sits the children alphabetically.

4. Donald doesn't get angry when the fourth grader says that the hat belongs to him. The fourth grader wanted to make Donald cry and he only smiles.

5. Donald loves school so much he arrives early and even goes one Saturday.

6. Donald believes the stars fall from the sky and his mother collects them using heavy gloves and sunglasses. Then she puts them in the freezer for forty-five minutes.

7. When Donald wants two stars, she gives him one and says when he really needs one during a bad day she will give him the other one.

8. Donald enjoys wearing the button so it is more punishment to him for her to keep it in the drawer.

9. Andrew doesn't come out of his room because he is angry about moving.

10. Donald loves saying funny sounding words and Snickerdoodles is one of the funniest.

Page 13

Accept appropriate speeches.

Page 14

You might have students correct each other's papers.

Page 16

1. Soccer is a game that never stops. It is a "free-for-all," as disorganized as Donald is.

2. Donald is not interested in winning. He just wants to have fun.

3. Donald scores the winning goal in the championship game, even though it is an accident.

4. To make Andrew feel better, Donald offers to give him his championship trophy.

5. Donald asks Mrs. Bidwell how many days are left in school and she thinks it is rude.

6. Donald throws up all over Mrs. Bidwell's prized and expensive board eraser.

7. The principal is angry with Mrs. Bidwell when she yells at Donald to leave school and he goes home.

8. Mr. Zinkoff cannot take Donald on his mailman route during a regular work day.

9. Mr. Zinkoff says "piece of cake" about the time he had to deliver the mail in an ice storm.

10. The Waiting Man has been waiting 32 years for his brother to return from the Vietnam war.

Page 18

1. Donald enjoys school since he gets there early and always has a positive attitude. He loves answering questions so he listens closely to what the teacher asks. One Saturday he gets up by himself and goes to school so he would rather be there than stay home. He loves to tell his parents what he does in school.

2. Mrs. Bidwell assumes Donald will be a problem and never changes her opinion. She wonders why she ever became a teacher. She thinks her eraser is more important that Donald's feelings.

Page 21

1. Donald has an operation to keep him from throwing up so much.

2. In order to keep Donald from leaving the house, Mrs. Zinkoff puts Polly by the door. If he tries to leave, Polly screams "bye-bye."

3. Donald fears the darkness of his cellar. He thinks the "Furnace Monster" lives down there.

4. Donald thinks he fails his test when he cannot touch the furnace and run back upstairs.

5. Since Mr. Yalowitz name is at the end of the alphabet he probably has had experiences of being forced to sit in the back of the room and he didn't like it.

6. The "big-kid eyes" notice that Donald is clumsy, volunteers for everything, has stars on his shirts, and even has a birthmark on his neck.

7. Donald loses the Field Day for the Purple Team when he runs the anchor leg too slow.

8. In 5th grade, Donald is "tagged and bagged" as a "loser."

9. Claudia's mother keeps her daughter on a leash.

10. Donald chooses Hector Binns since Hector also has no best friend.

Page 23

1. Donald knows his dad will "never giver up on him" when Mr. Zinkoff takes him for a ride the night after he loses the Field Day for the Purple Team. Mr. Zinkoff never drives the car when there is no place to go because it is a "waste of gas." But that night the two of them go riding to "no place in particular." Donald then knows that no matter what he does his dad will never think he is "a clunker."

2. Before the garage sale Mrs. Zinkoff asks Donald if it is all right to sells his old toys including his prized giraffe hat. This shows she respects her son's feelings.

Answer Key (cont.)

4

1. mouse
2. dog
3. eel
4. ox
5. bunny
6. bee
7. owl
8. bat
9. snail
10. lamb
11. mule
12. lark

Page 26

1. Donald shares his lunch, his allowance, and his candy. He also introduces him to Claudia and tells him about the Waiting Man.
2. Accept appropriate answers. One answer: they really don't have much in common. They are nothing alike.
3. Donald receives an ovation when he gets the only "A" in the class on a major test in geography.
4. Donald realizes that his dad is delivering mail to the old lady's house while he is hiding in there.
5. Donald is so upset about running away that he has to tell somebody about his troubles.
6. Donald sees graduation as a test because certain people get louder and longer cheers than others. It is a test of comparisons.
7. Polly yells for Donald and that is important to him to be recognized this way.
8. At first Andrew ignores Donald then he looks down on him and tries to make him feel bad.
9. Donald cannot play the flute and march at the same time.
10. Accept appropriate answers. One answer: No one pays any attention to Donald so it is as if he is not there.

Page 31

1. The police cars and emergency vehicles on Willow Street are there because Claudia has disappeared.
2. Donald holds on to his lucky stone to feel closer to Claudia as he searches for her.
3. As he searches for Claudia, Donald thinks of Polly since she, too, used to run away but was always found. Donald hopes he can find Claudia.
4. Donald is not the type to give up. That is one of his characteristics. He sets his mind to find Claudia and he is determined to do it.
5. If Claudia isn't found, Donald worries that her mother will turn into a person like the Waiting Man who sits in the window and stares.
6. Accept appropriate answers. One possible answer: Three experiences that happen to Donald as he is looking for Claudia are: his mind begins to wander, he falls down and goes to sleep, and he puts Claudia's 'stone' in his mouth.
7. Donald was found at one in the morning. Claudia had been found at eight in the evening.
8. Claudia's mother thinks Donald is a brave and wonderful boy because he tried to find Claudia and wouldn't give up.
9. The person who finds Donald is a man driving a snow plow.
10. Accept appropriate answers. One possible answer: Bonce sees something special in Donald. He admires Donald's positive attitude and refusal to give up.

Page 36

Accept appropriate answers. One example:

Incident: At the end of the novel, when Donald refuses to go home when the sides have been evenly picked and he is the odd person left.

In the open mind—words: happy, excited, want to play, want new friends, run, tackle, fun, pick me!, way to go, Donald!

Pictures: crossing the goal line with the ball, the others cheering for me, being tackled, running, jumping,

Page 43 Unit Test

Matching

1. e
2. f
3. h
4. c
5. g
6. b
7. d
8. a

True or False

1. True
2. False
3. False
4. False
5. False

Sequence

3-2-5-1-4

Paragraphs

1. Accept appropriate responses. Check to see that the writer cites specific characteristics of Donald's personality.
2. Accept appropriate responses. Check to see that the writer clearly explains how Donald feels.

Page 44

Accept all reasonable responses

Page 45

Perform the conversations (dramas) in class. Ask students to respond to the conversations in several different ways, such as, "Are the conversations realistic?" or "Are the words the characters say in keeping with their personalities?"